Contents

Introduction

The 5 Second Rule by Mel Robbins is a powerful motivational self-help book which reveals how five-second decisions and acts of everyday courage can change your life for the better!

According to Robbins, we have only 5 seconds to act on an instinct, impulse, or idea before we hesitate. If we wait longer than that, fear, doubt, or excuses are likely to creep into our mind, and more often than not, the action never happens.

To overcome this hesitation, everytime you notice an opportunity or get the urge to approach someone new, start an important task, or speak up in a meeting, you must count backwards from 5 to 1 and *act immediately*.

Mel Robbins discovered the 5 Second Rule at a time in her life when she was struggling with depression, endless worry, and crippling anxiety. Her marriage, finances, and career were at an all-time low.

Despite all of that, she managed to turn her whole situation upside down with the use of the Rule!

The Rule helped her reach her goals, break her bad habits, and become the greatest, happiest version of herself.

By applying the Rule, Robbins got rid of her tendency to hesitate, procrastinate and overthink. She became more present, productive, and self-aware. She also learned how to stop doubting and start believing in herself, her abilities and ideas.

And the best part is, The Rule can do the same for you! As you begin to use this ritual on a daily basis, you'll find that it doesn't take long before you're able to notice tremendous improvements in your personal and professional life!

This summary highlights the key ideas and captures the most important lessons found in the original book. If you've already read the original, this summary will serve as a reminder of main ideas and key concepts. If you haven't, don't worry, here you will find every bit of practical information that you can apply. However, we do encourage you to purchase the original as well for a more comprehensive understanding of the subject.

PART 1 – The 5 Second Rule

Chapter 1. Five Seconds To Change Your Life

Ways to use the 5 Second Rule:

• To push yourself to stick to your goals
• Become more influential at work
• Be more productive
• Step outside your comfort zone
• Become more efficient at networking
• Monitor yourself and control your emotions
• To manage, engage, motivate and encourage team members.

Every single day you find yourself facing moments that are difficult, uncertain, challenging, or scary. Your life demands courage. And that's precisely what The 5 Second Rule will help you discover—the courage to become your greatest self.

The Rule is centered around only one thing—YOU. Whether you're aware of it or not, there is greatness inside of you, and The 5 Second Rule will give you both the clarity to see that greatness and the courage to act on it.

The Rule will push you to honor your instincts and ideas with action so that they manifest themselves in the real world. And each time you use it, you're getting closer to becoming the person you're meant to be.

Once you start using the 5 Second Rule to push yourself out of your head and into action, you'll be amazed how easy it is to change your life, and you will finally realize that you are capable of accomplishing and experiencing anything that you dream about!

Chapter 2. How The Author Discovered the 5 Second Rule

Right before discovering the 5 Second Rule, things weren't going too well in Mel Robbins' life. She was facing serious problems related to money, work, and marriage. When the alarm went off each morning, she recalls feeling so dreadful and overwhelmed that she didn't even want to wake up and face the day ahead.

Then, one morning, she decided to break the habit. She still felt the same feelings that she had experienced for months: fear, dread, and anxiety.

In that particular moment, though, she noticed a tiny window of time in which she had a powerful desire to change her life for the better. There was a moment – a brief window of time – before her mind started to kill this positive thought.

So, she did something she'd never done before. The previous night, while watching a commercial, she remembers seeing a rocket launch into the sky. So she decided, what the heck, why not to just launch herself up like a rocket. Couldn't hurt.

And instead of hitting snooze again, she started counting backwards:

5-4-3-2-1...

And then... She stood up. She launched herself right out of bed, something she hadn't been able to do for months.

This was the exact moment that she discovered The 5 Second Rule.

She used the same countdown the next day, and it worked. In fact, it's worked every single time she's used it.

And then all of a sudden, she started to see these moments all the time, these five second windows.

So she made a promise to herself: If she had an instinct to do something that would improve her life, she would use this new rule to push herself forward, regardless of how she felt.

This is the essence of The Five Second Rule: The moment you have an instinct to act on a goal, you must push yourself to move within 5 seconds or your brain will kill it!

Chapter 3. What You Can Expect When You Use It

Mel Robbins used the Rule to get to the gym, to drink less, to look for a job, and to become a better wife and parent. Her husband, Chris, used it to stop drinking, start meditating, and exercise every day. And then, after gaining confidence and momentum through these seemingly small steps and achievements, they both used the Rule to climb out of debt and rebuilt themselves professionally, one 5 second push at a time.

As we can see, the 5 Second Rule does work like a charm to help you wake up on time or go to the gym, but its true power lies in how it helps you shake up your entire life. Using the Rule will strengthen the belief that you have the ability to control your own fate—because you're proving it to yourself one push at a time. As you use the Rule more and more, you'll begin to feel courage, pride, confidence, and a sense of control.

So, if there's *any* area of your life that you wish to improve, use the 5 Second Rule.

If you need more confidence, use the 5 Second Rule.

If you need motivation, use the 5 Second Rule.

If you are sick of doubting yourself, use the 5 Second Rule.

The Rule doesn't make things easy. But it makes them happen. That's why it's a tool. It's not advice. It's not something you think about. It's something you do. It requires instant action.

The moment you start thinking about something that feels difficult, uncertain, or scary, you hesitate. When you hesitate, you hold yourself back. Your brain believes you're in danger and triggers fear. But in order to accomplish your dreams or fulfill your desires, you need to move past that hesitation and fear. And the easiest way to do this is by using The 5 Second Rule. The Rule will push beyond hesitation – straight to action!

Chapter 4. Why The Rule Works

Motivation is merely an illusion. We've all bought into this idea that a constant feeling of motivation is what will finally push you to go after your big goals and most unreal dreams.

But the truth is, you're never going to feel like it. Motivation doesn't just come in an instant and stays for the rest of your life. Instead of approaching changing your life and accomplishing your bucket list like a huge task which requires constant motivation to keep you on track, you must start thinking about the small changes you can make, every day, that will create life-altering positive differences over time.

That's why the 5 Second Rule is essential to learn—it will be the push that you need in the moments when you don't feel like doing something, but know you should do it.

The 5 Second Rule is a form of metacognition, which means that it's a way of tricking your brain in order to achieve your greater goals.

By forcing yourself to take action instead of stopping to "think about it," you can create phenomenal change. Counting backwards to yourself does a few important things: It distracts you from your fears and worries, it focuses your attention on what needs to be done, it prompts you to act, and it breaks the habits of hesitating, overthinking, procrastinating, and holding yourself back.

In other words, the Rule allows you to beat your brain at its own game and distract it from the ways that it tries to sabotage you.

Most of us live our lives in autopilot mode. In fact, research has shown that 40% of our day is generally spent in autopilot. When we're on autopilot, we're operating solely out of habit.

And most of our habits are not necessarily serving us.

You see, your brain wants to protect you. It wants to keep you safe. It does this by keeping you from doing anything that feels scary, hard, or uncertain.

So, our default habits are usually doing what feels safe and easy. Our default habits are doing the same old things over and over – in our default habits, in autopilot mode, we are not living our greatness. We are stuck. And we're not improving.

And most of all, we feel a lack of control over our lives.

When you feel out of control, when you're living without a feeling of real control over your life and outcomes, your prefrontal cortex begins to malfunction.

The prefrontal cortex is really important–it's the part of the brain that's involved in things like planning, decision-making, and working towards goals.

To optimize the activity of your prefrontal cortex, you must take control of it. And you do this by creating a feeling of control in your life. This is where the 5 Second Rule comes into play.

When you count down from 5 to 1, you're taking a deliberate action. The countdown pushes you out of autopilot. And when you act, you're exercising control and you're turning on your prefrontal cortex.

By taking actions that make you feel in control of your life, your life will literally begin to change in every single way. As you use the Rule, you cultivate what researchers call an *internal locus of control,* which means that you believe you have control over your outcomes and future success.

Research shows us that those with an internal locus of control are happier, in better health, more likely to achieve at work, and have lower levels of anxiety and depression. And the more often you use the Rule, the easier it becomes to keep using it and keep feeling a sense of control over your life.

Why? The principle of *momentum.* It's the same in science and in psychology. Science proves that the initial amount of energy to start a reaction, the "activation energy," is significantly higher that the amount of energy re☐uired to keep it going.

Same in life. That activation energy re☐uired to get you going is really hard to come by, but when you use the Rule, you can push past your feelings of resistance.

And once you're using the Rule, it becomes much easier to keep making progress, thanks to the momentum which is propelling you forward.

Along with momentum, something else keeps you moving forward: *The Progress Principle.*

Research from the Harvard Business School has demonstrated that making progress, even in small ways, is the key to productivity and happiness.

The 5 Second Rule allows you to make progress every single time that you use it, which in turn leads to a better mood and increased productivity–which makes you more likely to keep using the Rule!

It's a positive feedback loop. And that's not the only positive feedback loop that the Rule creates.

Usually, you're locked into a negative feedback loop regarding your habits. For example, you have a habit of eating unhealthy, which in turn makes you feel guilty, yet you still have the urge to eat more. It's a negative spiral.

The thing is, you will always have that urge to engage in a negative habit. You're going to have the urge to smoke or skip a workout or procrastinate. And that's okay. Don't expect the urge to go away. You're not a failure for feeling the urge.

However, when you feel triggered to engage in the negative behavior, you can use the Rule instead to replace the negative action with something positive, and you will begin to create new behavioral patterns.

This is what researchers call *"the Golden Rule of Habits"* - it's replacing the negative behavior after an urge with something more positive and using the 5 Second Rule to help you take that positive action.

Soon, you'll be creating new positive habits which will boost your self-confidence and lead to lasting positive behavior change.

As your habits change and using the Rule becomes natural, you are now acting with something researchers call "*a bias towards action*" - instead of hesitation and procrastination, your default mode becomes one of taking action.

And the more action you take, the better your life becomes. This is a concept in psychology called "*Do Good, Be Good.*" It actually dates back to Aristotle. It's the idea that you can't just think yourself to change. You need to actually take action.

So now you're no longer thinking. You are doing. And doing changes your life.

By doing and accomplishing, you develop what is called "*authentic pride*" - the type of pride that is fueled by personal confidence and success. This feeling of authentic pride will be one of your biggest motivators when it comes to crushing your goals and moving forward!

With all the information provided above, you should now have a good understanding of WHY the 5 Second Rule works.

But *don't* spend much time analyzing or THINKING about it. You just need to start using the Rule and see the results in your own life. The 5 Second Rule is all about action.

So, every time you feel yourself shifting into autopilot, count 5-4-3-2-1 to bring awareness to your mind – and act immediately!

PART 2 – The Power of Courage

Chapter 5. Everyday Courage

As mentioned in the first chapter, everyday life is full of scary moments, uncertain, and difficult. Facing these moments and unlocking the joy, opportunity, and magic in your life re⊡uires tremendous courage.

Courage is exactly what the 5 Second Rule gives you. That's what courage is - a push. The kind of push that we give ourselves to stand up, show up, speak up, go first, step outside of our comfort zone, or do anything that feels hard, scary, or uncertain.

Courage is a birthright which lies within each and every one of us. You were born with it and you access it anytime you want. It's not really a matter of personality, confidence, education, status, or profession, but simply a matter of knowing how to find it anytime you need it.

Courage is the ability to take difficult or intimidating actions. It is the ability to take action in the face of self-doubt, fear, uncertainty, overthinking or hesitation.

Courage is an ability, just like lifting heavy weights is an ability. You increase strength by pushing your muscles, and you increase your "courage fitness" through consistent, daily acts of courage.

At first, it's hard to take courageous action. It's just like that first day at the gym. But as we push ourselves to exercise the muscle of courage, a funny thing happens. Every single time you flex it, taking courageous action becomes that much easier. Every time you push yourself to step outside of your comfort zone, speak up, wake up to face the day ahead of you or advocate for your needs, you complete a "courage workout."

Daily courage workouts lead to strong courage muscles, and that's when being courageous becomes a habit. In the moments when you face self-doubt, fear and hesitation, you can push past these feelings with ease. When your courage muscles are in tip-top shape, your feelings don't control you.

After a few weeks of consistently hitting the gym, exercise feels automatic, and your courage muscles work in the same way. But when you stop working out, your physical and courage muscles will atrophy. Doctors recommend daily exercise for your health. I recommend daily acts of courage for your soul.

It's in the moments in which you push through hesitation using courageous actions that you change your life. When you take control of a situation with an act of everyday courage, you are no longer defaulting to fear.

In moments of hesitation—those times when your feelings of doubt and worry and fear creep in—you have a critical opportunity. It's the opportunity to practice everyday courage. Where you once needed to courageously push yourself to overcome hesitation, you will now find it to be second nature.

Chapter 6. What Are You Waiting For?

Are you waiting for the next time? Waiting for right time? Waiting to feel ready? To feel worthy? To be good enough?

Well, keep in mind that often there is no "next time," no second chance. There's no "right time" to improve your life. Stop waiting - it's either now or never.

When you wait, you aren't simply procrastinating. You're doing something far more dangerous - you are deliberately convincing yourself that "now it's not the time." You are actively working against your dreams.

When you make excuses or talk yourself into waiting because you're afraid of failure or rejection, you are limiting your potential to make your goals and dreams a reality.

The difference between those who make their dreams come true and those who don't is simple: those who fulfill their dreams have courage to start and the discipline to keep going. The 5 Second Rule is a total game-changer because it forces you to get out of your head, start taking action, and keep moving forward.

When you apply the Rule to push yourself forward, you see the magic in your life and you open yourself up to the possibilities and opportunities that surround you.

Sure, sometimes things might not work out the way you want them to – you might not get the girl, the part, the job, or the response you expected – but that's not the point. The point is to gain something far more important — the courage to pursue your dreams, and the go-getter mindset which will allow you to succeed in the long run!

Chapter 7. You'll Never Feel Like It

In case you've ever wondered why it's so damn hard to make yourself do something that you know will solve your problems or improve your life, here's the answer: it's your feelings.

We may not realize it, but we all tend to make decisions that are based on feelings, not on logic.

Sure, we all like to believe otherwise – that we're very sensible creatures who rely on logic when making decisions, but that's rarely the case. According to neuroscientist Antonio Damasio, it's our feelings that decide for us 95% of the time. We feel before we think. We feel before we act. And that's how we ultimately make decisions—based on how we feel.

Change is hard. Logically, you might know exactly what you should do, but your feelings about doing it will likely have a bigger impact on your decision.

But the fact is, how you feel in the moment is almost never aligned with your goals, dreams, and vision of the future. If you only act when you feel like it, you will never be consistent enough to get what you want.

You must learn how to separate your feelings from your actions. Take a look at the best-performing athletes, for instance. Ever wonder how they manage to achieve so much? Well, part of it is talent and practice, but another key element is the ability to detach from their emotions. They may feel tired, but they keep running. They may feel the pressure, but they keep a cool head. They know feelings cloud their judgement, and they choose to ignore them.

Fortunately, this kind of mental resilience is a *skill* – one you can develop by applying the 5 Second Rule and forcing yourself to act. If you don't feel like attacking the to-do list on your desk, you won't, but by applying the Rule, you can shift the focus away from how you feel and move it towards what you must do.

You may not be able to control how you feel, but you *can* control how you act.

Chapter 8. How To Start Using the Rule

Using the 5 Second Rule is simple: start by counting backwards to yourself: 5...4...3...2...1. The counting will help you focus on the task or goal and distract you from the fears, thoughts, and worries in your mind. Then, when you get to "1," *move*. That's it.

The easiest way to jumpstart your use of the Rule is by doing a simple *Wake Up Challenge*. Just set your alarm for tomorrow morning 30 minutes earlier than usual, and the moment it starts ringing, count 5...4...3...2...1 and push yourself out of bed.

Here's why this challenge is really important:

1. The challenge is very straightforward, so there's no wiggle room. It's just you, the alarm clock, and a 5-second interval. You know exactly what you need to do, and you're fully responsible for the outcome - if you fail, it's only your fault and nobody else's.

2. If you can change your morning routine, you can change anything. Change and improvement require you to act deliberately, no matter how

you feel. If you can master that skill in one area of your life, you'll be able to apply it in other areas as well.

3. You'll experience a concept called *"activation energy"* and realize how hard it actually is to push yourself to do simple things. Chemists have found that the activation energy of a chemical reaction - the initial amount of energy required to ignite it - is much higher than the average amount of energy needed to keep the reaction going. And just like in chemistry, the initial amount of energy that you need to push yourself out of bed is way higher than the energy you exert once you're up and moving.

This first bout of activation energy will feel so uncomfortable, but if you *do* manage to get up the moment your alarm rings, you will feel a huge rush of energy and personal power. This one simple act of getting out of bed when the alarm goes off demonstrates that you possess the inner strength to do what needs to be done and helps you start the day on a positive note.

After conquering the Wake Up Challenge tomorrow morning, you can start using the 5 Second Rule to:

• Change your behaviour. Use the Rule to push yourself to create positive habits, pull yourself away from the destructive ones, and exercise self-control.

• Control your mind. The 5 Second Rule will stop the endless barrage of worries, anxieties, and negative thoughts that weigh you down.

• Act with everyday courage. By applying the 5 Second Rule, you'll discover the courage that you need in order to do things that are new, uncertain, or scary. The Rule will quiet your self-doubt, and as you push yourself to pursue your goals and passions, you will gain tremendous amounts of confidence.

PART 3 – Courage Changes Your Behavior: How to Become the Most Productive Person You Know

Chapter 9. Improve Your Health

Improving your health is all about action. Pretty much every single diet, meal plan, exercise program, weightlifting routine, meditation technique or yoga flow will improve your health, as long as you STICK TO IT.

Whatever your health goal may be — losing weight, burning fat, building muscle, improving strength, eating healthier, lowering cholesterol, or healing yourself from illness — you can use the 5 Second Rule to get it done.

All you have to do is pick a plan that fits your goals, and force yourself to follow through.

The only choice you'll need to make after picking your plan is the choice of DOING WHAT YOU HAVE TO DO every single day, even though you really don't feel like it.

And every time you slip or fall off the wagon, remember — it takes just 5 seconds to get back on track.

Chapter 10. Increase Productivity

FOCUS is the essence of productivity. There are 2 types of focus that you need in order to be highly productive:

1. The ability to manage distractions and remain fully focused on the task at hand.

2. The habit of focusing on what's truly important to you in the long run, so you don't waste your day on stupid or unnecessary stuff.

Get serious about managing distractions – first you must acknowledge the fact that distractions and interruptions of any kind are not good for productivity (social media, cluttered workspace, constantly checking your emails, the colleague who keeps bugging you over nothing, and so on). Then you take measures to remove them, or you limit your access to them. It's that simple. With no distractions around, with less interruptions to your train of thought and action, you'll be able to focus strictly on the relevant things that matter and your productivity will increase tremendously.

Big picture focus – own your mornings. How we wake up is just as important as we sleep. Taking control of your mornings is a game-changer for productivity. Create a morning routine that helps you focus on your long-term as well as your short-term goals, tasks, and priorities. Customise it to your needs, include some planning time for the day ahead. Add some form of exercise or meditation. Create a routine that you can do every single day, and do it as soon as you jump out of bed.

Chapter 11. End Procrastination

Procrastination is not a problem per se. When working on creative or innovative projects, research shows that procrastination is not only unavoidable, but also desirable. The creative process requires time and inspiration, so your mind needs to wander, a.k.a. to procrastinate. That extra time spent mental wandering often allows you to come up with ingenious or creative ideas that are beneficial to your project. In other words, those fresh new ideas that you get as you procrastinate will improve the end product of your work – this is *productive* procrastination.

Destructive procrastination, on the other hand – is when you avoid the work that you need to get done and *know* there will be negative consequences. For a long time, many people believed that procrastination was synonymous with laziness, poor time management skills, a lack of willpower, or lack of self-discipline. Procrastination is *not* a form of laziness, though, but a coping mechanism for stress. We procrastinate because we feel stressed out, not because we're lazy.

Procrastination is like emotional binge eating for the mind. When you avoid something that feels stressful or hard, you get a brief sense of relief. Furthermore, when you do something you enjoy, like browsing on Facebook or laughing at viral videos, you get a short-term dopamine boost. And the more often you procrastinate, the more likely you are to repeat the behavior. But here's the problem: While you might be getting small boosts of relief when you're watching funny cat videos, over time the work that you're avoiding builds up. This creates more stress in your life, which in turn leads to even more procrastinative behavior, and so the cycle keeps repeating itself.

So how do you stop this vicious cycle? By simply applying the following steps:

1. Forgive yourself for procrastinating. This may sound silly, but part of the problem that psychologists have uncovered is that procrastinators are really hard on themselves to begin with. Most procrastinators report feelings of shame and guilt every time they procrastinate. Those feelings increase their stress, which leads to even more procrastination and less productivity. So, every time you catch yourself procrastinating, forgive yourself – you've become aware of your behaviour, so now you've got the chance to assert yourself and take control over the situation. This leads us to Step 2.

2. Every time you catch yourself procrastinating, just ask yourself "What would the *Future Me* do?" Dr. Pychyl from Carleton

University has been doing a lot of research on our *"present self"* (the person we currently are) vs. our *"future self"* (the person we want to become). He found that when we picture our *future selves,* our current actions become more in tune with what we want to obtain in the long run.

3. Get started with the 5 Second Rule. Once you understand the source of your procrastinative behaviour and acknowledge what your future self would do, it's very important to get started. Telling yourself to "just make the damn call, finish the task, reply to the email" and then taking action is the secret to completing anything important. As explained throughout the book, the Rule switches the gears in your mind and activates the prefrontal cortex which will make it easier for you to get started. And each time you use it, it will get easier and easier to stop procrastinating and get going.

P.S. In order to beat the habit of procrastination effectively, remember to start small. Eat the elephant one bite at a time. For instance, the author recommends working on something you've been avoiding for just 15 minutes at a time. Then, feel free to take a small break and do something enjoyable if you need to. You're only human after all.

PART 4 – Courage Changes Your Mind: How to Become the Happiest Person You Know

Chapter 12. Stop Worrying

More than any other change, getting rid of your habit of worrying will create the biggest positive impact in your life.

As adults, we spend way too much energy and time worrying about things we cannot control or which could go wrong. This creates unnecessary stress and robs us of enjoying and savoring the present.

Worrying is a default setting that your mind reverts to when you're not paying attention. We all have this tendency to drift into worry, at least from time to time. The key is catching yourself as soon as you do it, and then using the Rule to regain mental control.

When your mind tries to take you somewhere dark, sad, negative, or doubtful, you don't have to go with it. Use the 5 Second Rule to regain command of your mind, and then replace the negative thought with a positive one.

If, in that 5 second window, you cannot come up with something positive, simply ask yourself: "What am I grateful for in this moment?"

That simple question forces you to focus on the positive aspects of your life. As soon as you *think* about what you are grateful for, you will start *feeling* grateful as well and your feelings of worry will vanish.

Chapter 13. End Anxiety

Anxiety occurs when your habit of worrying goes out of control.

The key to overcoming anxiety is *understanding* it. If you can catch it right as it kicks in, you'll be able to reframe it, preventing it from escalating into full blown panic – this is known as *anxiety reappraisal.*

When you feel anxious, you get into a state of physical and mental agitation. Your adrenaline surges. Your heart starts racing. Your palms start sweating. Your breath speeds up. Your whole body goes into a state of hyper awareness, preparing itself to fight or flee any danger that may arise.

That's why telling yourself to calm down when you're anxious doesn't really work – you can't just go from 100 to 0 mph in an instant.

You must redirect the anxious energy instead. Use the 5 Second Rule to assert control over your mind and then *reframe* the *anxiety* as *excitement* so that your brain doesn't escalate it to panic.

This is easier than it sounds like, because anxiety and excitement are two sides of the same coin.

Physiologically, anxiety and excitement are the exact same thing. They both put your body in a state of arousal, preparing it to take action. The difference is only psychological.

In the case of anxiety, your mind focuses on possible dangers, risks or obstacles – this leaves you feeling tense, uneasy, and uncertain.

In the case of excitement, however, your mind sees an opportunity or a potential reward – this leaves you feeling confident, invigorated, and motivated to take action.

As you can see, it's all about perspective.

So, instead of saying you feel anxious about something, say you feel excited and repeat it until you believe it!

But remember: Telling yourself "I'm excited!" does not immediately lower the feelings of adrenaline surging through your body, but it *does* channel those feelings in a positive direction, giving your mind an explanation that encourages and empowers you to take action.

Chapter 14. Beat Fear

This chapter reveals how Mel Robbins managed to cure her long held fear of flying with the use of *anchor thoughts*.

So basically, before she begins her trips, Robbins visualizes the exciting things she'll get to do once she arrives at her destination (such as climbing Table Top mountain with her friends, or taking a wonderful walk along Lake Michigan with her mom).

And then, everytime she gets nervous on the plane, she uses the 5 Second Rule to flush the fear out of her head and she forces herself to focus on the positive images that she visualized right before the flight.

By using these anchor thoughts, she is constantly keeping her eyes on the prize, which helps her remain calm during the flight.

You can use this technique to overcome any kind of fear. Every time you're dealing with a fearful situation, simply create an anchor thought by visualizing a positive outcome of that situation. That thought will keep you grounded, focused, motivated, and even excited.

PART 5 – Courage Changes Everything: How to Become the Most Fulfilled Person You Know

Chapter 15. Building Real Confidence

Many people wrongly believe that confidence is just a matter of personality and that "you either have it or you don't." But the truth is, anyone can learn how to become more confident.

Confidence simply means that you believe in yourself, your abilities, and your ideas. It is not an innate personality trait, but a skill you can acquire through a series of small decisions and daily acts of courage – such as speaking up in meetings, working on those tasks or projects that you keep postponing because you "don't have time," approaching that girl or guy you like, or signing up for something you usually wouldn't.

In other words, doing things that scare you or require you to get out of your comfort zone on a daily basis will *surely* raise your confidence. The more you apply the 5 Second Rule and push yourself to act when you're afraid, speak when you're nervous, or go to the gym when you don't feel like it, you realize you have the power to get anything done. You build a real sense of pride, confidence and control over your life, which keeps growing and growing with every step you take.

Chapter 16. Pursuing Passion

This might sound like a cliché, but most people struggle to follow their passsions because they don't listen to their heart.

To find your true passion, all you need to do is pay attention to your instincts, to the things that truly move you, and then use the 5 Second Rule to push yourself to explore those things as soon as you've become aware of them.

Your instincts signal what your heart really cares about. If, all of a sudden, you find a new thing or subject that you can't stop thinking about, don't hesitate to turn it into a hobby. Take simple steps to explore it: read about it, talk to others about it, watch tutorials, take a class, and write a plan to turn it into a project. You will be surprised by what happens over time.

Your passion will start as just an instinct, a hobby. And then momentum builds up. First you take a class. A class leads to certification. Certification leads to connections. Connections lead to opportunities. Small opportunities lead to larger ones.

And all of a sudden, you realize your passion project is becoming a passion-driven business or career, creating major positive change in your life and allowing you to be the greatest, happiest version of yourself!

P.S. Always remember that you're never too old to discover and pursue your true passion.

Chapter 17. Enrich Your Relationships

Mel Robbins' advice regarding relationships is simple: *Just Say It! Leave nothing important unsaid.*

In other words, whenever you feel the urge to say something important to someone you care about, count backwards from 5 to 1 and force yourself to say it.

Yes, being intimate or emotional often requires courage, but we have to understand that waiting for the right time to get real in our relationships is rarely a wise move – that time may never show up.

There's no *right time* to ask the hard questions, have that conversation, express your feelings, or take the time to truly listen. There is only *the here and now.*

And if you don't do this as soon as your heart demands it, you might never get the chance to.

Millionaire Mindset Summaries

Millionaire Mindset Publishing provides the greatest self-help, business, psychology, and personal development books summarized for your convenience.

Our summaries aim to teach you important lessons in a time-efficient and cost-effective manner. They are coherent, concise, and comprehensive, highlighting the main ideas and concepts found in the original books. Unessential information is removed to save the reader hours of reading time. You can check them out at:

www.amazon.com/author/millionaire mindset

Also, if you enjoyed this summary, please take a minute of your time to leave a review on Amazon.com. It will be tremendously appreciated!

Thank you and good luck!

Made in the USA
Middletown, DE
19 September 2018